自信

Social Emotional and Multicultural Learning | Non-Fiction Series

Copyright © 2022 by Level Learning, INC. and Washington Yu Ying PCS™
Original and Edited Text Copyright © 2022 by Washington Yu Ying PCS™

All rights reserved. No part of this book in whole or part may be reproduced without written permission from the publisher.

Published by Level Learning, INC.

Content Contributors:
Washington Yu Ying PCS™
Level Learning - Ya-Ching Chang

Illustrations by: Josh Taira

Leveling classification based on Level Learning standard. For full description, visit www.levellearning.com

ISBN 978-1-64040-085-6
Simplified Chinese Edition

About Level Learning:
Level Learning provides a literacy focused curriculum specifically designed for K-12 Chinese as a Second Language classrooms. Our program offers 20 levels of specific and detailed objectives, leveled texts and passages, mastery-based online assessment, and analytics to enable data-driven instruction. Level Learning reading curriculum for both literature and informational text emphasize grammar and comprehension skills to help teachers develop confident and independent Chinese language readers. The non-fiction series of books are specifically designed to support our informational text course based on multiple national standards. To learn more about our entire offering, visit www.levellearning.com.

About Washington Yu Ying PCS™:
Washington Yu Ying PCS is a Mandarin English dual language immersion International Baccalaureate (IB) World school. Yu Ying's mission is to inspire and prepare young people to create a better world by challenging them to reach their full potential in a nurturing Chinese/English educational environment. Yu Ying's comprehensive IB, dual immersion curriculum equips students with global competencies for success in the real world. As a leader in immersion education, Yu Ying is determined to advance Chinese language programs and global citizenry education by helping other schools create and strengthen their Chinese programs. For more information, email: products@washingtonyuying.org

美国作家爱默生说过:"自信是成功的秘诀。"为什么自信这么重要呢?

因为自信会让人对自己充满希望。有自信的人敢于面对挑战，解决问题，成功就会变得容易。

没自信的人不相信自己的能力。他们不敢尝试挑战，遇到困难就放弃，这样就很难成功。

7

其实，自信不是天生的，我们可以多练习。试试下面的方法，让自己变得更自信吧！

第一，学会相信自己。告诉自己："继续努力，我就会成功！"学会相信自己，我们就会发现，其实成功一点儿也不难。

第二，保持积极的心态。告诉自己："每个人都会遇到困难，只要努力克服，接下来就会变得简单。"保持积极的心态，克服困难一点也不难。

第三，学会面对压力。在其他人给自己压力时，告诉自己："做最好的自己，不用在意别人的看法。"学会减轻压力，让自己快乐起来一点儿也不难。

另外，学会欣赏自己也是自信的一部分。写下自己的进步和长处，或是成功时给自己一个奖励。

自信的人，懂得相信自己、欣赏自己。自信的你一定会取得成功！

Glossary

	Pinyin	English Definition
美国	měi guó	United States
作家	zuò jiā	author
爱默生	ài mò shēng	Emerson (Ralph Waldo Emerson)
自信	zì xìn	self-confidence
成功	chéng gōng	success
秘诀	mì jué	secret
重要	zhòng yào	important
充满	chōng mǎn	fill with
希望	xī wàng	hope
敢于	gǎn yú	to have the courage
面对	miàn duì	face
挑战	tiāo zhàn	challenge
解决	jiě jué	to solve
相信	xiāng xìn	believe
能力	néng lì	ability

	Pinyin	English Definition
尝试	cháng shì	to try
遇到	yù dào	to encounter
困难	kùn nan	difficult
放弃	fàng qì	to give up
天生	tiān shēng	born with
继续	jì xù	to continue
保持	bǎo chí	to maintain, to stay
积极	jī jí	positive
心态	xīn tài	mentality
克服	kè fú	to overcome, to endure
压力	yā lì	pressure
在意	zài yì	to care about
减轻	jiǎn qīng	to reduce
欣赏	xīn shǎng	to appreciate
取得	qǔ dé	to obtain

www.ingramcontent.com/pod-product-compliance
Lightning Source LLC
Chambersburg PA
CBHW041223070526
44584CB00001B/72